ALGRAV GUID

CW01429586

Embark on an Unforgettable Adventure, Discover Must-See Places, Immerse Yourself in Rich History, and Soak in the Culture of the Algarve in 2024!"

Marsha M. Buckwalter

Table of contents

INTRODUCTION

Discover how to get to the Algarve.

The Algarve region of Portugal is a stunning location that may be visited in a variety of ways. With its bright Mediterranean environment and kilometers of sandy beaches, it's no surprise that millions of people visit this famous region each year. Traveling to the Algarve may be a fantastic experience.

If you prefer a road trip, you may explore Portugal's countryside and breathtaking 800-mile coastline at your leisure. Renting a car or riding the bus are popular ways to travel by land. Take a ferry from Spain for a one-of-a-kind experience while admiring the magnificent sea vistas. Alternatively, the train provides comfortable seating with attractive village and hillside views. Whatever path you choose, you will embark on an exciting adventure.

Arriving in the Algarve Region of Portugal By air.

One of the most common ways to come to the Algarve is by plane. Faro Airport (FAO) is the primary gateway into Portugal from Europe and other parts of the world. The airport is near Faro Beach, which offers spectacular views and a variety of activities for holidaymakers who want to explore once their flight has arrived. Visitors to Faro Airport can take busses or cabs directly to their accommodation or transfer to public transit, including trains and buses, to carry them farther inland. When guests arrive in the region, they have a variety of lodging alternatives, including luxury hotels, resorts, guesthouses, and even camping sites in Lagos and the surrounding surroundings. Hotels near Faro Airport are especially useful since they provide quick access to the city core and neighboring beaches without incurring transit expenditures or delays.

Exploring Algarve:

When it comes to experiencing the stunning coastline of the Algarve, the best vantage point is from above! Whether you're arriving by car, sea, or train, the allure of this Portuguese gem awaits, promising sun-drenched beaches, delectable cuisine, and unforgettable adventures.

By Car: Hit the Open Roads For those craving the freedom of the open road, two major highways, the A22 (Via do Infante) and A2 (Auto Estrada Lisboa-Algarve), seamlessly guide you into the heart of the Algarve. Begin your journey in Faro, where the city's charm invites exploration before venturing further south. Car rentals from Faro Airport provide flexibility, allowing you to navigate Portugal's breathtaking landscapes at your own pace, with pick-up and drop-off options conveniently scattered across the Algarve.

A scenic drive unveils Portugal's captivating coastline, offering a perfect blend of adventure and beauty.

By Sea: A Seafarer's Dream Embark on a remarkable maritime adventure by opting for a cruise or ferry to the Algarve. A ferry ride from Ayamonte in Spain to Vila Real de Santo Antonio in the Algarve promises a 15-minute journey surrounded by the soothing embrace of ocean breezes and panoramic coastal views. Step aboard for a cruise, setting the stage for an unforgettable exploration of the Algarve's pristine beaches.

By Train: Tranquil Travels Traveling to the Algarve by train unveils the countryside's beauty and provides a chance to connect with fellow travelers. While there are no direct trains from outside Portugal, arriving at Porto or Lisbon Airport sets the stage for a scenic train ride. The journey from Lisbon to the Algarve takes approximately four hours, offering glimpses of the picturesque landscapes. For those heading north to Porto, express trains streamline the journey, taking about six hours without intermediate stops.

However, you choose to reach the Algarve, an exciting escape filled with sun, sea, and unique experiences awaits. With easy accessibility, planning your trip to this Portuguese paradise has never been more convenient. So, why wait? Start planning your Algarve adventure today!

What to Pack for Your Algarve Trip

Embarking on a journey to the sun-kissed shores of the Algarve requires thoughtful packing to ensure you're fully equipped for a memorable and comfortable adventure.

1. Lightweight Clothing: Pack light, breathable fabrics to stay cool in the Mediterranean climate.

Comfortable shorts, sundresses, and T-shirts are perfect for daytime explorations. Don't forget a swimsuit for the beautiful beaches and resort pools.

2. Sun Protection: Sunscreen with high SPF to shield your skin from the intense sun. Sunglasses and a wide-brimmed hat for added protection. A lightweight, long-sleeved shirt for cooler evenings.

3. Footwear: Comfortable sandals for strolling along sandy beaches and exploring charming towns. Sturdy walking shoes for more adventurous activities and hikes.

4. Travel Essentials: Valid passport, travel insurance, and any necessary travel documents. Electrical adapters for your devices, as Portugal uses the European standard. A compact umbrella for unexpected showers.

5. Health and First Aid: Personal medications and a basic first aid kit. Insect repellent to ward off any pesky mosquitoes.

6. Technology and Entertainment: Camera or smartphone for capturing the stunning landscapes. E-reader or books for relaxed moments by the pool or on the beach.

7. Beach Essentials: Lightweight beach towel for lounging by the water. Beach bag to carry your essentials. Snorkeling gear if you plan to explore the underwater beauty.

8. Cultural Etiquette: Modest clothing for visits to churches and cultural sites. A scarf or shawl for covering shoulders when required.

9. Dining Out: Smart-casual outfits for dining at upscale restaurants. Reusable water bottle to stay hydrated in the warm weather.

10. Daypack: A small daypack for daily excursions, carrying water, snacks, and your essentials.

11. Miscellaneous: Travel-sized toiletries to save space in your luggage. Portable charger for your devices to keep them powered throughout the day.

CHAPTER ONE

Getting around the Algarve

Getting around the Algarve is easy and cheap, especially if you choose to use public transport. Each mode of transportation has different advantages depending on your needs and budget.

Car

The most convenient way to travel about the Algarve is by automobile. This is the fastest way to get to cities and beaches. Some of the more remote beaches are only accessible by car.

The Algarve has two main road leading to important cities.
The A22 motorway is the fastest route. You have to pay a toll to drive on this road. Most rental cars have an electronic device that records your journey on the A22.

The rental company takes the costs automatically.

The second road is highway N125. It's a highway you can drive for free. If you want to hang out and enjoy the scenery, this is the best choice.

Car Rental

If you have not driven your car to the Algarve, we recommend renting a car. It is more expensive than traveling by public transport, but if you value speed and freedom over cost, renting a car is a great way to travel and get around the Algarve. There are several different car rental companies in the Algarve, each with its pros and cons.

Bus

Bus is operated by three bus companies in the Algarve region: § Próximo § Eva § Frota Azul Algarve Tickets are purchased at bus stations and it is recommended to have (small) cash to pay for the tickets. Bus stops are marked with the Paragem sign. In the most important cities, both
Portuguese and English signs are used: paragon/bus stop.

Buses stop at every stop, but when waiting for a bus and seeing a bus approaching, it is recommended to signal the bus driver. Catch a ride on Bus 16 for a convenient trip from Faro Airport straight into the heart of Faro City! If you arrive at Faro Airport and want to take a bus to Faro, you should take bus 16. The city's local bus company is called Próximo. The buses are recognizable by their light blue and white pattern. The price of a single ticket is €2.25. The journey from the airport to the city center bus station takes about 20 minutes.

The bus makes several stops, including a stop at the main shopping center Forum Algarve. The bus runs twice an hour and the bus connection is daily. Intercity buses The bus takes you to all the most important cities in the Algarve. Most long-distance buses in the Algarve are operated by bus company Eva. The buses can be recognized by the white, orange, and green patterns. Please note that the buses do not have routes/route numbers. You have to check the destination screen on the front of the bus. The destination can be written on a piece of paper attached to the driver's window. In the Portimão area, some buses are operated by the bus company Frota Azul Algarve. Tickets and prices Bus tickets can only be purchased at bus stations.

Just to paint a picture of the cost for you, we have listed the prices of individual tickets from Faro to several popular destinations:

Albufeira: €4.90 $

Lagos: €6.20 §

Portimão: €5.75 §

Olhão: € 3.40 $

Tavira: 4. 444 50 €

The tourist pass is an easy and cheap way to travel between all the cities of the Algarve. With the pass, you can use the EVA Transport and Frota Azul Algarve bus network unlimitedly.

The prices are § 3 days: €30.40 , 7 days: €38.00 Most buses operate from 07:00 in the morning to 10:30 p.m. There is less bus traffic on weekends than on weekdays. In many smaller rural villages, there is no bus service on weekends or holidays. Major long-distance bus routes have weekend and holiday traffic but operate less frequently.

Train

The name of the railway company organizing the train traffic is Comboios de Portugal (CP). Between Lagos and Vila Real de Santo António, there is a railway that connects the west of the Algarve with the east. The train conveniently stops at several key urban hubs, including Lagos, Portimão, Albufeira, Loulé, Faro, Olhão, Tavira, and Vila Real de Santo António, offering travelers access to these vibrant destinations.

Note that train stations are not always located in city centers. For example, in cities like Albufeira and Loulé, the train station is located a few kilometers from the city center. These are the Algarve regional train stations: Tickets and prices You can buy train tickets online from the Comboios de Portugal website, saving you money. If you buy your tickets in time, you can

get a discount of up to 65%. You can travel by express train (IC) or regional train (R).

Below are the prices of single tickets to Faro to give you an idea of the costs:

Albufeira:

€9.50 second class; €11.50 first class

§ R: €3.35

§ *Portimão*

  § IC: €12.55

  § R: €10. 55

Lagos € second class 44 A great economic option is to buy a tourist travel card. With this card, you can travel by train on Algarve Line Regional trains for 2 or 3 days in a row.

The prices
- are: 2-day ticket

- § adults €20.90

- § children €15.90 3-day ticket adults €31.90

§ children €23.90, Travel ticket €44.

Taxi Driving a taxi is a convenient and fast way to get around the Algarve. Especially if you don't want to travel abroad, this is a great transportation option. Taxis operate day and night and carry up to four passengers. When you give a cab company a ring to book a ride, you can order a larger vehicle. All taxis have a meter and it depends on the distance and traffic how much it costs. The purpose is to mention that the price between the airport and the city of Faro is 10-15 euros. The trip takes about 15 minutes. The price from the airport to Albufeira isaround 55 euros.

This trip takes about 40 minutes depending on traffic.

Uber

Uber has conquered the transport
market in the world. In the Algarve, it is also very
* popular with tourists and locals alike. It's an easy way to get around cities.

The main benefit is that you don't need cash, the costs are automatically charged to your credit card.

Exploring the history and culture of the Algarve region

The Algarve is a stunningly beautiful European destination that has attracted visitors from all over the world for centuries. From the stunning beaches and untouched beauty of the Algarve to its rich cultural heritage and unique traditions, the Algarve has something to inspire everyone.

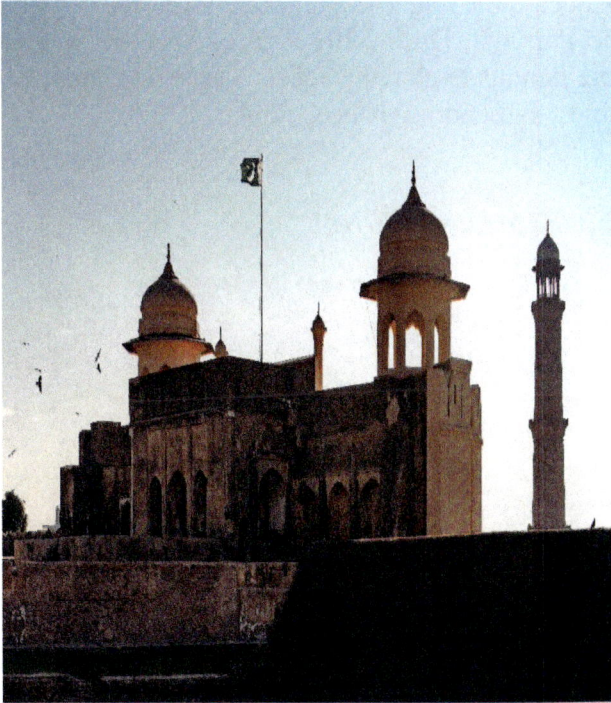

A Brief History of the Algarve Region of Portugal

The Algarve attracted early settlers, starting with the Phoenicians, who established trading posts and introduced olives, grapes, and fig trees. The Romans, who arrived in the 2nd century
BC turned the area into a thriving commercial and agricultural center. Later rulers included the Visigoths and Moors left a lasting legacy of castles and fortresses. In 1249, King Afonso III of Portugal conquered the Algarve from the Moors and began to rule Portugal. During the Age of Discovery, there were famous explorers such as Vasco da Gama, Gil, earnes, and Pedro Alvars Cabral

Visit the Medieval Silves

Castle in Algarve, Portugal, and witness the magnificence of a time gone by. This time of investigation was driven to riches, empowering the development of invigorated towns, churches, and religious communities within the locale. The 20th century marked a critical change within the Algarve locale of Portugal, as tourism developed as a major industry beginning in the 1960s. Nowadays, individuals from all over the globe come to savor the sunny climate and breathtaking coastline of the Algarve.

With a history traversing thousands of long times and a wealthy social legacy, there's much more to find past its beautiful shorelines amid your Algarve travel! Investigating the Interesting Culture of Algarve, Portugal The Algarve locale of Portugal grandstands its wealthy history through an assortment of social treasures traversing from Roman ruins to Moorish design. Also, the locale brags lovely churches and cathedrals eminent for their building style and chronicled significance.

But the Algarve's dynamic.Portuguese culture isn't restricted to its momentous landmarks. The nearby individuals epitomize the region's profound social roots and cherished conventions. They warmly welcome guests and eagerly share their traditions and legacy, taking monstrous pride in exhibiting their domestic to travelers. Investigate the Algarve's wealthy culture through music celebrations and conventional movie exhibitions. Submerge yourself within the region's culinary conventions, savoring dishes like caldeirada (angel stew) and pastéis de bacalhau (codfish cakes) passed down through eras.

Visit Faro's Cathedral within

The Algarve and explore its grand magnificence and centuries-old history. Speaking of great nourishing food, did you know that the Algarve region of Portugal is domestic to a few of the world's most scrumptious wines? It's genuine! The Algarve locale has long been known for its productive generation of full-bodied white wines made from inborn grapes, such as Arinto and Siria grapes, as well as strong reds made from Trincadeira or Moreto grapes.

In case you need to dig into the soul of things, why not take a visit around a few neighborhood Algarve wineries? Doing so will not as it were permit you to test a few delightful neighborhood wines but will moreover let you discover all about the intriguing world of wine generation. Taste the most excellent of Portugal's Algarve locale with a visit to one of its numerous wineries. So why not make your other trip one filled with revelation?

Head down south to Portugal's sunny Algarve locale and encounter firsthand all it has to offer. From old ruins to conventional food – and so much more – there's something here within the Algarve to charm everybody.

CHAPTER TWO

The ideal time to visit the Algarve.

The Algarve's golden, cliff-backed beaches are among the most beautiful in Europe. Given the region's evident natural beauty, as well as the excellent surfing, kayaking, and other aquatic activities, it's no surprise that southern Portugal attracts large people.

Although temperatures fluctuate by month, the Algarve receives consistent sunshine for 300 days every year. Summertime sees the most people, while winter feels more local, although there are lots of activities going on regardless of when you visit.

Until recently, many resort towns in the Algarve were virtually closed for the winter, leaving few options for housing, restaurants, and planned trips.

That has changed in recent years, as the Algarve Tourism authority has moved to promote the region as a year-round resort.

Nonetheless, certain places remain closed for the season, so bear this in mind when making your plans. Here's our advice on the ideal times to visit the Algarve.

June-August is the finest period for excellent weather.

During high season, the Algarve sizzles, promoting days of relaxing on the beach followed by refreshing dips in the ocean (cool Atlantic currents prevent the sea from becoming as warm as it does in the Mediterranean). During the summer peak, there is also little rainfall and almost little cloud cover. Festival season begins in June, and the entire region joins in.

The hottest months in the Algarve are July and August. the average temperature is roughly 28°C (82°F), while occasional days can reach 40°C (104°F). With mild ocean breezes, nighttime temperatures hover about 22°C (72°F), ideal for comfortable alfresco dining. In July, music events on the beach, such as Afro Nation Portugal in Portimão, and a candlelit culture fair at Mercado de Culturas à Luz das Velas in Lagoa, attract large crowds.

The hot August temperatures make it ideal for a refreshing dip in the cool Atlantic waves. It's also an excellent month for spotting dolphins on a boat trip. The Portimão street food carnival and Olhão seafood festival provide opportunities to meet locals and sample wonderful local cuisine.

Naturally, the peak tourist season corresponds with these enticing beach conditions. Hotel prices are at their greatest, and crowds have reached their pinnacle. If you intend to travel during this time, you should make your plans well in advance. Expect to spend a premium to get your preferred accommodations. You'll also have to share those beautiful sands with a lot of other travelers – April to May and September to October are the times to enjoy outdoor activities.

If you enjoy hiking, horseback riding, mountain biking, and other land-based sports, the best months to visit are April to May and mid-September to October. The days are still bright and sunny, with just a slight probability of drizzle, and the temperatures rarely get to the point of discomfort. Easter in April generally signals the end of the off-season in the Algarve, with the region's dormant seaside resorts resuming activity. Easter processions are exciting, as is Liberation Day (April 25), which includes pyrotechnics and parades in some towns.

Whether you're embarking on a big trip like the 300km (186-mile) Via Algarviana or simply going for a seaside walk in the afternoon, the sunny, rain-free month of May is ideal for being outside. During the Kizomba Open Summer Festival, Albufeira will host day parties and dance workshops; don't miss out on the opportunity to dance until dawn with an an incredible roster of international musicians.

Water temperatures in September are nearly identical to those in August, but colder air temperatures provide for enjoyable beach days. There will be fewer crowds than the prior month. At the Flamenco Festival in Lagos, you may perfect your strut under the sun. Birdwatchers flock to the Algarve in October to view winged beauties passing by.

It's also a good month for outdoor activities, as you get a welcome break from the summer heat.

During this period, there are significantly fewer people and compared to the high season, you can save up to 30% on accommodation prices. April and May are also good months to see wildflowers on the hillsides, fields, and coastal areas of the Algarve.

November to March is the best time for a short visit The Algarve feels like a different place when you travel in the off-season. You'll see far fewer crowds and hear far more Portuguese everywhere you go. The temperature drops, but the days are still quite pleasant, with an average temperature of about 16 °C (61 °F), even in the coldest weeks of January and February.

Although most of the Algarve's annual rain comes in winter, the showers are usually short and you re likely to see plenty of sunny days.

As the days get shorter in December, you will experience harsh night temperatures but nice mild days with maximum temperatures around 17°C (62°F). Before Christmas, many towns have special markets and a life-size nativity scene (Vila Real de Santo António is one of the biggest in Portugal).

The cultural calendar of the Algarve includes many art exhibitions, dance and theater performances, and special winter films in January. Faro, Portimão, Lagos, Loulé, and

Albufeira are the most active, as well as Tavira and Silves.

On cold February evenings, locals go indoors to watch live music and dance performances in larger cities. Since there are usually no tourists, the days in the seaside towns are quite quiet, except during the carnival celebrations, when there are parades and parties in the streets.

The early days of spring in March bring longer days and the first flowers to the hills of the region. With pleasant temperatures, March is ideal for long walks without the crowds.

All in all, high season in the Algarve is still a good time to be outside, although imagine long walks by the sea instead of swimming in the sea (a light jacket is handy).

Top 10 Apartments in the Algarve

If you are going on holiday to the Algarve, there are many great apartments to stay in. What are the best homes away from home? We have created the best accommodations where you can relax, have plenty of space, and enjoy your vacation to the fullest.

These are the 10 best apartments in the Algarve.

1. **Luna Solaqua (Albufeira)**

Are you planning to stay at the most famous resort in the Algarve? If you want to live in Albufeira, your best apartment choice is Luna Solaqua. These spacious 60 square meter apartments have a balcony, a flat-screen TV, and a private bathroom with free toiletries and a hairdryer.

The well-equipped kitchen includes a microwave, toaster, fridge, and kettle. The air-conditioned rooms ensure that you feel cool on warm Algarve evenings. In addition, you can refresh yourself in the beautiful outdoor pool. Free internet access and free private parking make it perfect.

2. Salgados Vila das Lagoas (Albufeira)

If it can never be big enough for you, choose Salgados Vila das Lagoas in Albufeira. Two-bedroom apartments are 100 square meters and three-bedroom apartments are 134 square meters. The modern apartments have 2 bathrooms, a large living room, a kitchen, a balcony, and free Wi-Fi. In addition, the apartments are part of a resort with 7 outdoor pools, a restaurant, and a bar.

The farm is surrounded by a beautiful green garden with olives and palm trees, creating a peaceful haven in this bustling city.

3. Aparthotel Vila Luz (Luz)

Aparthotel Vila Luz Located near Praia da Luz in Lagos, these stunning beachfront apartments offer panoramic views of the Atlantic Ocean from a cliff set amongst stunning landscaped gardens.

The light-filled studios are 50 square meters and offer just the amount of space and comfort you would expect from a home away from home. In addition, the apartment has a terrace or a balcony, depending on the level. The resort has a swimming pool, a garden, and a bar where you can enjoy late-night drinks. The hotel has free internet access and free private parking.

4. Sagres Time Apartments (Sagres)

There is no comparison to Sagres Time. For a truly wonderful   holiday, you must travel   to   the most south-western point   of   the   Algarve and reach the peaceful town of Sagres.

In this wonderful place, you will feel the greatness of nature and the legendary history that makes it a magical place. At Sagres time apartments, you can stay in spacious one or two bedroom apartments with large balconies offering stunning views of the Atlantic ocean.

Some apartments have a garden terrace with direct access to an outdoor heated saltwater pool.

The fully furnished apartments are air-conditioned in summer and heated in winter, making them ideal accommodations all year round.

5. Pestana Alvor Park Hotel Apartment (Alvor)

In the lively beach town of Alvor, you can have a great stay in the Pestana Alvor Park Hotel apartments. The spacious apartments are 65 square meters and have a balcony and a kitchen with everything you need.

The resort also has a restaurant, so there is always a chance to enjoy breakfast there. For recreation, you can take a bath in the indoor and outdoor pools, or enjoy a Turkish sauna or a massage. Kids have both an indoor play area and an outdoor play space to enjoy. Parents can also use babysitting services.

6. Residences at Victoria at Tivoli (Vilamoura)

If you're looking for luxury, stay at The Residences at Victoria's exquisite apartments in upscale Vilamoura. This is one of the most luxurious apartments in the Algarve. Known as Monaco of Portugal, Vilamoura is for the rich and famous and admirers of the super-rich. The large two and three-bedroom apartments (130 square meters and 150 square meters) are designed to make you feel at home with marble floors, beautiful kitchens, and large living rooms.

The air-conditioned apartments offer panoramic views of the lush surroundings and guests have exclusive access to the outdoor pool at Palms Resort by Anantara Vilamoura.

7. La Canopée (Tavira)
Tavira is often regarded as among the prettiest towns throughout the Algarve region. If you want to have an authentic experience and live like a resident of Tavira, La Canopée is your perfect home away from home. This two-bedroom apartment stands out from the crowd thanks

to its stunningly stylish interior and romantic roof terrace.

Love is in the details and the hosts make sure you feel welcome right away, stocking the fridge with local food and drinks. Located in a quiet street but a short walk from the city center, this private apartment is the best choice for a relaxing holiday with plenty of space for the whole family.

8. Water Green House (Portimão)

Portimão is a popular holiday destination, especially around Praia da Rocha. Near Praia da Rocha you will find the Water Green House, the perfect place for a holiday in the Algarve. This elegantly furnished one-bedroom apartment can accommodate up to 4 people. The fully furnished apartment is bright and airy and has a sea view from the balcony. The top floor has access to a private pool. There is also an underground garage where you can park safely.

9. Quiet Village (Carvoeiro)

Quiet Village is the perfect place to stay in the colorful beach town of Carvoeiro. The well-designed apartments are located in a green and peaceful environment, within walking distance of the beautiful beaches and extraordinary rocks of Algar Seco. You can choose between one-, and three-bedroom apartments with a very elegant living room with a fireplace and balcony.

The apartments are very spacious: 100 square meters and 120 square meters. Compared to other apartments in the Algarve, it offers excellent value for money. Guests can swim in the outdoor pool or relax on the sun loungers.

10. (Faro)
Stay in the heart of Faro and live like a local in André's wonderful home. This bright apartment is 82 square meters and has 2 bedrooms, tiled floors, a living room and dining room, a good modern kitchen, two balconies, air conditioning, and internet. It is an ideal base for exploring the historic city of Faro, the surrounding beaches, and the beautiful Ria Formosa Natural Park. Guests love the location, the romantic decor, the cleanliness, and the interaction with the host who will ensure you have the best vacation experience.

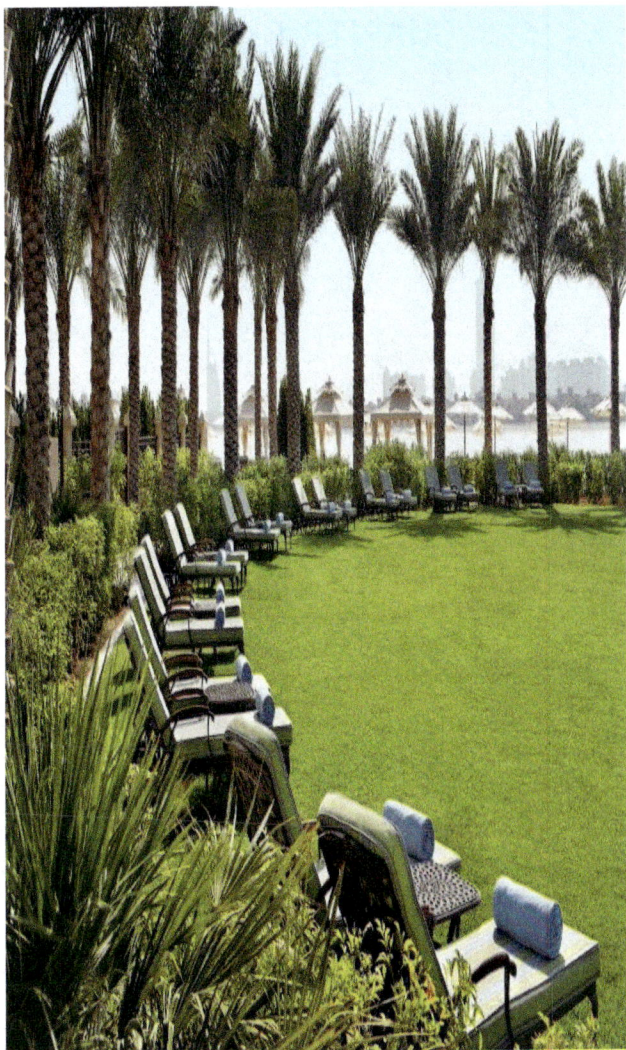

CHAPTER THREE

Algarve Facts

If you want to come to the Algarve, there are a few things you need to know before we start our list of the best things to do and see in the Algarve.

The Algarve is a beautiful large region covering approximately 5,000 square kilometers of the coast of southern Portugal.
• The main entrance to this area is Faro Airport, which is the international airport of the area.

• There is a direct train service from Lisbon that conveniently stops at Albufeira and Faro. There is a high-speed train between the two cities and the journey takes about 3 hours.

• If you want to travel by road, FlixBus is available and offers connections to other cities.

• The most popular cities in the Algarve are Faro, Albufeira, Vilamoura, Lagos, and Portimão, each with its unique charm and stunning views.

• Consider renting a car for ultimate flexibility, especially if you plan to visit the many resort towns dotted along the coast. But UBER is also available in the Algarve.

Top 25 Things to do in the Algarve

1. *Visit Benagil Caves*

Inside Benagil Beach which is empty and crowded. The famous Benagil Cave, also known as Algar de Benagil, has a remarkable hole in the ceiling that creates a natural skylight that illuminates the sandy beach inside. This is a must-see for anyone visiting the Algarve region.

The cave itself is close to several popular Algarve destinations. Lagos is just a 45-minute journey from here, while you can reach Albufeira in about half an hour. Portimão also isn't too far; it's a mere 45-minute drive away.There are also several ways to visit the caves, including bus, car, public transport, or an excursion such as a boat trip or kayaking.

Note that the cave is crowded, especially in the summer season (or low season), so if you come, try to come either early in the morning or in the evening. Many tours offer either sunrise or sunset, like this First Inside Benagil cave tour.

2. Have lunch under 2000 olive trees

Of course, the Algarve has its share of sun, sand and beaches. But take a little trip inland for a unique treat – the chance to enjoy lunch and wine under a 2,000-year-old olive tree at Morgado do Quintão Estate.

Located between Silves, Monchique, and Lagoa, this family business has been growing grapes for around 300 years. It was founded in the 19th century by Count Silves. Today it is one of the best quality wineries in the Algarve.

The estate itself organizes several experiences, including lunch or dinner under an olive tree, as well as wine and vineyard tastings. They also sell their wines on the property, offer spa treatments, and even rent cabins if you want to stay a while.

I had the pleasure of having lunch at Morgado do Quintão Estate and had the best time

3. Tandem Skydiving Algarve

Are you ready to see a different view of the Algarve? Try this tandem skydive. It starts with a 20-minute flight over the beautiful coast. When you reach 15,000 feet, you and your pilot jump out of the plane.

You experience approximately 70 seconds of free fall before landing safely on the soft sandy beaches of Portimão. Embarking on a skydiving journey offers a one-of-a-kind perspective of the Algarve as you soar through the skies. This incredible experience also includes all the necessary equipment and safety instructions.

4. Seven Hanging Valleys Hike

Also known as Percurso dos Sete Vales Suspensos, The Seven Hanging Valleys Route voted one of the best hikes in Europe by Top Destinations Europe, is a scenic route that runs from Praia da On the eastern side, you'll find the Marinha, but if you head over to the western shoreline, there's the stunning Praia de Vale Centeanes waiting for you.

This is a popular, easily accessible route with a section of wooden walkway that takes you through typical dry Algarve vegetation, over golden pebble beaches, cliffs, and unique rock formations of the Algarve coast.

The trek itself is about 11 km and takes about 6 hours to complete. A reasonable level of fitness is recommended for comfortable participation. The trailhead entrance is 5-10 minutes by car or taxi from the town of Carvoeiro.

The track can easily be completed on your own. However, there are also many tours like one on land and sea 7 hanging valleys roads plus 2-hour cruises or this one from olhao.

5. Coastal and cliff jumping in Lagos
Are you looking for an adventure full of adrenaline in the Algarve? Consider

this excursion near Lagos. With a small group, you will travel to a beach set on high cliffs and be prepared for a day of exciting outdoor activities.

Here you can climb jagged cliffs, jump off cliffs, swim in azure seas, explore hidden caves, and discover sheltered beaches in a few action-packed hours. This trip takes you to places that are usually off-limits and offers a unique perspective on the Algarve.

The tour includes convenient transportation from Lagos, all necessary equipment, and expert guidance, ensuring a safe and unforgettable experience.

6. Visit Castro Marim and enjoy a mud bath

Travel back in time by visiting the charming historic town of Castro Marim in the southeastern corner of the Algarve, right next to the Spanish border. The landscape is dominated by salt ponds, wetlands, a medieval castle from the 13th century, and a fortress from the 17th century.

As you stroll around the town, you're welcomed by pristine white homes, ancient fortifications, quaint cobblestone lanes, and delightful little plazas. Besides its stunning landscapes and incredible historic buildings, this small town is known for one more thing: Spa Salino Água Mãe.

5000 years ago, salt was already produced in the salt pans of Castro Marim. Today, these salt pans are known for having the purest salt crystals in the world. They also offer a unique mud spa experience that is truly
one of a kind.

Here people can float in the mineral water of these salt areas, apply salt clay to their body, or
enjoy the spa's most important therapeutic and relaxing massage. You will also learn about the centuries-old process of making salt.

7. Surfing

The Algarve has around 200 kilometers of stunning coastline, which means plenty of opportunities to have fun in the water. If you're looking for more than just a relaxing day at the beach, I recommend surfing.

If you are looking for surfing, the west coast of the Algarve offers bigger surf, cooler temperatures, and wild nature. Great places are Praia da Bordeira and Praia do Amado. However, surfing lessons can be taken almost anywhere in the Algarve - including Faro, Albufeira, Portimão, and Lagos.

8. Eat seafood in Olhão

Cataplana Algarve is Algarve seafood cooked in a special box-shaped pan. It contains seafood, vegetables, and spices perfectly cooked.

Travel to Olhão, a gem of the Eastern Algarve known for its lively fish market and Moorish-inspired architecture. At this spot, age-old customs embrace the ocean, creating a haven for those who loves seafood. Here, local fishermen bring in the day's catch and deliver the freshest ingredients to the city's famous fish restaurants. However, Olhão is not only about the sea. Walk through the old town and you'll find charming cobbled streets lined with traditional cube-shaped houses. Characteristic flat roofs and an outdoor staircase show the North African influence of the area.

If you want a unique experience in this small fishing village, book today Morning - Beach Breakfast or When the sun goes down - Sunset Picnic (for at least two people)

For nature lovers, Olhão is the entrance to the Ria Formosa Naturalisse Park, a labyrinth of islands, lagoons, and swamps full of wild animals, which brings me to the next activity.

9. Cruising through the Ria Formosa Natural Park

View of Fuzeta, a former homestead in the municipality of Olhão, Portugal Journey to the Ria Formosa Natural Park (Parque Natural da Ria Formosa), a magnificent labyrinth of lagoons, marshes, and barrier islands extending 60 kilometers along the Algarve coast from the outskirts of Faro to the city of Olhão.

This remarkable nature reserve is a unique oasis full of diverse nature and especially a paradise for bird watchers, where hundreds of different species visit throughout the year.

In the heart of the park, five barriers - Barreta, Culatra, Armona, Tavira, and Cabanas - protect a vast lagoon system with clean beaches and quaint fishing villages accessible only by boat. Each island has its unique charm

10. Try Oysters In Culatra

If you're looking for a secluded experience, look no further.

Ready to enjoy the   best   oysters of your   life? I took this tour and although it was my first time to enjoy oysters, everyone in the group agreed that they were the best they had ever had.

Welcome to Culatra, an island in the Ria Formosa Natural   Park,   home   to   a close community of about 900 people, all united by a common life by the sea.

As you step onto the island, you will be introduced to   local shellfish   vendors who will   give   you an insight   into   their   sustainable   harvesting techniques. You   will also   meet   Silvia,   the dynamic president of the island. He steered the community toward a cleaner,

plastic-free environment, with a special focus on caring for young and older residents.

Through his works and anecdotes, culatra is protected from mass tourism and becomes a genuine sanctuary

11. Go see dolphins

The best way to see dolphins is on a tour like this Seafar cruise.
Embark on an exciting Seafar cruise from Lagos, Alvor, or Portimão, giving you a rare opportunity to see wild dolphins on the wide Atlantic.

The Algarve coast is a center of rich marine life, including a particularly thriving dolphin population. Species such as the common dolphin, bottlenose dolphin, and even the occasional visiting killer whale can inhabit these waters.

This thrilling ride on a rigid inflatable raft ensures close encounters with these playful creatures as they jump and slide through the waves. Don't forget to bring your camera to capture this unique marine spectacle with a 95% dolphin success rate.

12. Go on a classic food tour in Lagos

Embark on a journey through Lagos to explore the sumptuous tastes of the Algarve with our traditional culinary excursion. During the three hours, you will have the opportunity to visit four separate local eateries to taste up to 10 traditional Portuguese dishes with a local drink. For lovers of the morning tour, there is an additional stop at the lively city market Mercado in Lagos.

Expertly guided by locals, this tour takes you through charming narrow streets and immerses you in the history and culture of the area. Besides tasting authentic food, you can also find architectural gems and hidden stories there.

This guided tour is an excellent introduction for those discovering the Algarve for the first time and will provide you with valuable information to fully enjoy your visit to this beautiful part of Portugal.

13. Visit Praia Da Coelha

Explore Praia da Coelha (Rabbit Beach), a small but wonderful beach located on the south coast of the Algarve - 5 km west of Albufeira. Surrounded by striking cliffs and lush vegetation, this hidden cove is a paradise for those looking for a quiet beach holiday away from the typical tourist hustle and bustle.

Golden sand and crystal clear water Praia da Coelha offers great natural beauty and plenty of swimming, sunbathing, and beach activities. A nearby path along the cliffs offers stunning views of the Atlantic Ocean, making it a must-visit for nature lovers and tranquility seekers.

This is a great a family beach with safe, sheltered water and seasonal lifeguard services.

14. Spend a day at Praia Da Marinha

Located near the town of Lagoa (near Benagilia), Praia da Marinha is known for its stunning caramelcolored rocks, intricately formed by erosion against clear turquoise water.

The beach itself, the golden sand between these formidable cliffs, offers a peaceful haven for sunbathing, while the crystal-clear waters are perfect for snorkeling. Perhaps the most characteristic feature of Praia da Marinha is the double M-shaped arches in the rock face.

Whether you're navigating cliff-top hiking trails, swimming in azure waters or relaxing on a sandy beach, Praia Da Marinha is an unforgettable part of the Algarve's natural beauty.

15. Enjoy the beauty of Ponta Da Piedade

Welcome to Ponta da Piedade, the natural spectacle of Lagos, central to all Algarve Portugal routes. Known for its impressive sandstone cliffs covered in hidden caves and sparkling turquoise waters, Ponta da.

Piedade is a haven for those seeking natural beauty. There are 4,444 different boat tours available that offer close encounters with these geological wonders, while hiking trails offer stunning panoramic views from the top of the cliffs. It is a must-see destination for nature lovers and photographers in the Algarve.

16. Diving

One of the best places to dive in Portugal is in the Algarve. The Atlantic coast is considered one of the cleanest in Europe. It also has one of the largest artificial reefs in Europe - perfect for diving.

There are many reef dive sites and wrecks in the Algarve. You can also dive from all major cities including Lagos, Faro, Sagres, Portimão, and Albufeira.

One of the best places to dive is Ocean Revival Park. Four warships of the Portuguese Navy were deliberately sunk in the same place to create an artificial reef. It is known as one of the best diving destinations in Europe. Please note that you need an advanced open-water license to dive.

17. Ride a Jeep Safari with a Distillery Visit and Lunch

One of the stops is in Serra de Monchique

Embark on an adventurous Jeep Safari that takes you straight into the heart of the hidden landscapes of the Algarve, especially the fascinating Serra de Monchique.

Your route will take you through unspoiled areas and you will follow rustic roads through the untouched views of the Algarve. Small whitewashed villages line your path. The highlight of your adventure is a visit to a local distillery, where you can taste medronho, a strong local brew, and witness traditional honey-making practices. End your trip with a sumptuous lunch served at a classic local restaurant

18. Take a photo of Algar Seco

This is the view from Doll, but remember that this is a popular place with the best view, but you may have to wait. little

Have you heard of Algar Seco? It's only a 15-minute walk from Carveoiro and is home to quite the Instagrammable spot.

Algar Seco Carvoeiros is like a natural playground created by the sea. Millions of years of erosion have transformed the cliffs into caves, rock pools, and windows that look straight out to sea. One famous place, "Boneca" or "La Pupo", is a small cave in the rock that used to look like a doll. From inside this cave, you can see the sea.

This is a   small space and   there may be
a lot of people waiting to take pictures, so take your
time.

19. Walk the Carvoeiro Boardwalk
A wooden boardwalk stretches along the top of the
cliffs leading to some of the most beautiful beaches.
The   Carvoeiro   Boardwalk   is   a
wooden boardwalk that follows the coast and offers
great views of the sea and the cliff. The wooden
walkway starts in the town of Carvoeiro and
ends in Algar Seco.

Take a leisurely walk around this spot to soak up the
stunning views of the Atlantic. Make sure to bring
your camera along; you'll find countless moments to
capture. Whether it's the early morning glow or the
evening dusk, this boardwalk is an ideal spot to
appreciate the allure of the Algarve scenery.

20. Visit Cabo De São Vicente
Cabo de São Vicente, in the western Algarve, was
once considered the edge of the world.

Step into the edge of the world at Cabo de São Vicente in southwest Portugal. Steeped in maritime adventures and ancient maritime legends, this historic landmark was sacred ground to the Romans, who named it the Promontorium Sacrum.

Cabo de São Vicente, the westernmost point of the Algarve, offers a wonderful view of the vast Atlantic.

The site is home to an impressive lighthouse, It stands as one of Europe's mightiest, still steering vessels through the perilous shoreline currents. The nearby Fortaleza de Sagres guards the coast and offers a glimpse into the region's rich history.

21. Discover Vila Real De Santo António
Say hello to Vila Real de Santo António, a charming town located right on the border between Portugal and Spain. Its charming charm lies in its tree-lined squares, marina, and timeless 18th-century architecture.

A visit here takes you back in time, from the majestic Pombaline buildings to the iconic 19th-century obelisk that stands proudly in the Plaza Marquês de Pombal. In addition to the rich history, local cuisine can be enjoyed in seaside restaurants and cafes.

For a pleasant shopping experience, explore the citys many small shops and lively daily markets. Finally, you can walk along the guardiana river to see spain

22. Visit the Octopus Capital: Santa Luiza

If you like octopuses, visiting this resort is a good idea.

Santa Luzia is called the "octopus capital" because of its long tradition of octopus fishing. Local fishermen have developed unique octopus fishing techniques that have been passed down from generation to generation. The village is known for its abundant octopus fishing and the exceptional dishes that local chefs create from this marine animal.

In addition to its fishing opportunities, Santa Luzia exudes authentic Algarve charm with its narrow cobbled streets and charming traditional houses.

Additionally, Santa Luzia is close to the wonderful beaches of Terra Estreita and Barrili, adding beach charm to its quaint village charm.

23. Explore Roman ruins
Milreu Roman ruins

The Romans left behind some remarkable ruins in the Algarve. One place worth noting is the Roman ruins of Milreu (Ruínas Romanas de Milreu) near Esto, which have well-preserved ruins of a Roman villa with elaborate mosaics, baths, and a temple.

Cerro da Vila in Vilamoura stands out as a notable site from Roman times, where you can explore the remnants of an ancient fishing settlement, complete with a bathhouse, and even a museum on-site. Plus, if you're keen on delving into the Roman legacy of the area, don't miss out on the Roman Bridge in Silves, known locally as Ponte Romana de Silves, and the Roman Villa in Abicada, just a stone's throw from Portimão. Both spots offer a real glimpse into the region's storied past.

24. Swim At Praia Da Falésia

Praia da Falésia (also known as Beach of Cliffs) is one of the Algarve's longest beaches. The beach, which stretches over 6 kilometers long, is famed for its red and orange sand cliffs. Its natural beauty and relatively calm sea conditions make it a great place for swimming and water activities.

25. Visit Sudoeste Alentejano E Costa Vicentina

Looking for a more peaceful Algarve getaway?A great place to do this is Sudoeste Alentejano and Costa Vicentina

Sudoeste Alentejano and Costa Vicentina is a great choice for those looking for natural beauty, a clear coastline, and a more relaxing experience in the Algarve.

This area on the southwest coast of Portugal is characterized by spectacular cliffs, pristine beaches, and a protected natural park. It offers opportunities for hiking, bird watching, and enjoying the untouched landscapes.

The charming towns of Zambujeira do Mar, Odeceixe, and Sagres are worth exploring, and you can find charming beaches such as Praia da Arrifana and Praia do Amado. Sudoeste Alentejano and Costa Vicentina are a haven for nature lovers and those looking for a quieter coastal experience away from bustling tourists.

Algarve FAQs: What You Need to Know

- ***What's the Algarve Famous For?***
The Algarve is celebrated for its breathtaking coastal scenery, pristine beaches, and bustling
tourist scene. It's a place where you can marvel at dramatic cliffs, swim in turquoise waters, and bask in the gentle climate. This region boasts lively
resort towns, top-notch golfing, thrilling water activities, and quaint fishing hamlets. You can also discover historic sites, enjoy scrumptious seafood, and immerse yourself in the Algarve's friendly culture and traditions.

- ***Should I Visit the Algarve?***

The Algarve is a must-visit destination! It's brimming with diverse attractions and Experiences designed to delight all types of explorers.

- ***When's the Best Time to Visit the Algarve?***

Choosing the best time for an Algarve getaway hinges on what you're after. If you love the heat and a buzzing beach vibe, aim for the summer months, from June to September. For a quieter visit, the shoulder seasons of spring (April to May) and autumn (September to October) are ideal, offering mild weather and fewer tourists.

For those who enjoy cooler days and want to explore beyond the shore, winter (November to February) can be appealing, though it might be too chilly for a swim.

- ***Which Town Should I Stay in When Visiting the Algarve?***

Lagos is a prime spot to set up camp in the Algarve. Nestled in the western part of the region, it's a treasure trove of scenic beauty, historical allure, and a buzzing ambiance. Lagos is home to gorgeous stretches of sand like Praia Dona Ana and Meia Praia . its also a great starting point for excursions to must-see spots like Ponta da Piedade, Praia da Rocha, and Sagres.

- ***How Long Should I Spend in the Algarve?***

To savor the essence of the area, plan for at least 3 to 5 days. This gives you enough time to wander through various towns, lounge on the shores, and sample the local flavors. But if you're eager to uncover more hidden gems, take day trips,
or dive into activities like golf or water sports, consider staying for a week to 10 days.

Albufeira is often considered the Algarve's most tourist-centric town. Nestled in the heart
of the Algarve, it draws countless visitors with its well-developed tourist
facilities, lively nightlife scene, and a plethora of attractions catering to holiday makers.

CHAPTER FOUR

Exploring the Algarve

The Algarve beckons as an ideal spot for those in search of fun and adventure, and hitting the road is the quintessential way to take in the region's splendor. From its stunning coastline to quaint resort towns and hidden gems, the Algarve offers a little something for all tastes.

Set sail on a boat trip to admire the dramatic limestone cliffs, take a stroll on Tavira Island's sandy expanses, and enjoy the sight of orange groves scattered across the landscape. A short drive will bring you to unique dunes and the chance to savor fresh produce at a Saturday morning market.

Whether opting for a plush hotel stay or to seek out the Algarve's secret spots, there's an activity to delight every kind of traveler. Seize the chance to discover this magnificent region, with all its key sights and attractions, for an unforgettable retreat.

Top 10 Algarve Destinations

The Best Cities to Visit in the Algarve

1. *Lagos*

Boasting one of Europe's most stunning coastline, Lagos is steeped in history. Its breathtaking natural wonders, characterized by golden cliffs and extraordinary rock formations, have become a Portuguese highlight, thanks to social media. A network of beautiful beaches is accessible on foot, while others can be explored via boat or kayak. Catering to a diverse crowd, including surfers, families, and couples of all orientations, the charming Old Town is dotted with alfresco dining spots and hosts significant attractions like one of the Algarve's most opulent churches and a museum that delves into the history of the Atlantic slave trade. Lagos serves as an ideal base for venturing into the Algarve's western reaches, though its main attractions and beaches can be enjoyed in a day or two.

2. *Carvoeiro*

Although small, Carvoeiro is a fantastic base for beach enthusiasts. Its beach is a sight to behold, but the surrounding area is home to some of Portugal's top beaches, including the stunning Praia da Marinha. It's also the gateway to the famed Benagil Cave. The town appeals to a wide audience. From young couples to families and experienced tourists. Delicious restaurants and vibrant nightlife.

3. *Albufeira*

Known for its vibrant party scene, Albufeira is a hotspot for sun-seeking European youth who
enjoy the nightlife as much as the beaches. With a diverse range of splendid beaches, from hidden coves to expansive sandy shores, Albufeira is the Algarve's tourism hub. It boasts the largest selection of beaches lodging options to suit every pocket. The Old Town retains the allure of its fishing village past, with its white buildings and pedestrian-friendly streets.
Family-friendly water parks, top-notch golf courses, and luxurious resorts are all nearby, offering relaxation and entertainment.

4. *Faro*

As the Algarve's largest city and home to the international airport, Faro is often bypassed by beachgoers, who miss out on its charming walled town and intriguing monuments. The nearby natural park features a string of islands with pristine beaches that remain relatively undiscovered. Faro is perfect for those who appreciate a mix of culture and seaside relaxation, and its central location makes it an excellent base for exploring the entire Algarve and the Ria Formosa Natural Park's islands.

5. *Tavira*

Tavira is the Algarve's most enchanting town, preserving traditional architecture and
featuring an attractive Old Town with white churches and castle ruins. It's also the starting point for trips to the Ria Formosa Natural Park's islands,

which boast some of Portugal's finest beaches. The journey there takes you through wetlands teeming with wildlife. Tavira is ideal for those who prefer a more laid-back atmosphere and unspoiled natural surroundings.

6. Sagres

At the south western most point of Portugal, Sagres is where ancient Europeans once believed the world ended. The sense of standing at the edge of the world is palpable at the Cape of St. Vincent and the windswept promontory near this tranquil town. Prince Henry the Navigator's fortress still stands, Marking a significant historical site in the Algarve. The area's beaches draw surfers, and Sagres marks the start of the Costa Vicentina, an untouched stretch of coastline that's among Europe's best-kept secrets. The town exudes a bohemian vibe, with often empty beaches except for surfers and naturists. The local microclimate is cooler and less sunny than the rest of the Algarve, but the stunning scenery, magical sunsets, and refreshing sense of escape more than compensate.

7. *Portimão*

Portimão, a significant port city, may lack the quaint charm of other historic towns but has become a beloved tourist spot thanks to its beaches framed by impressive rock formations. Praia da Rocha is the largest and most famous, with a skyline that brings to mind Miami rather than a traditional Portuguese town. Heading west toward the old fishing village of Alvor, you'll find a succession of smaller, cliff-backed beaches. The scenery becomes more picturesque and tranquil as you approach Alvor, culminating in some hidden beaches of extraordinary beauty near the pine-covered headland of João de Arens.

Conveniently, hotels are often just a short walk away.

8. *Loulé*

Loulé, located inland, doesn't attract as many tourists as the coastal towns, but it's a popular day trip destination known for its renowned market and 13th-century castle. It's worth making a detour to the nearby town of Almancil to see the Church of St. Lawrence, adorned with exquisite baroque tiles.

Loulé is a worthy addition to any Algarve itinerary for those interested in local culture beyond the beaches. Plus, it's close to two of Europe's most opulent beach resorts, Quinta do Lago and Vale do Lobo.

9. Vilamoura

emerged in the latter part of the 20th century as one of the largest resort towns in Europe, rapidly transforming into a trendy hangout that attracts stars looking for first-class service. Today, while still upscale, it caters to a broader audience, offering the allure of having all amenities close at hand, right next to the beach. The town developed around a massive marina, one of the largest in Southern Europe, bustling with activity day and night due to the surrounding eateries, bars, and hotels. Although it's a hit with families, Vilamoura mainly appeals to adults with its trendy seaside bars, the Algarve's biggest casino, and some of the finest golf courses in Europe. Lacking historic buildings, the town does boast an archaeological site and museum showcasing a Roman settlement with well-preserved mosaics.

10. Silves,

Once the Moorish capital of the Algarve, saw its importance wane after 1755 earthquake and even earlier when Faro rose to prominence. Now a tranquil

town, Silves draws visitors to its impressive castle—the largest and most well-maintained in the region—often on day trips from Lagos or Albufeira.
Wander the cobblestone streets to discover a quaint Gothic cathedral and an archaeological museum, offering a delightful respite from the sun-soaked beaches.

Top beaches to see

When it comes to stunning beaches, the Algarve coastline stretches over 200 kilometers and is dotted with amazing rock formations, vast dunes, secluded coves, and tranquil islands. With over 150 beaches to choose from, the Algarve has been recognized as the top beach destination in the world.

To experience the finest, consider these recommendations:

- ***Praia da Marinha*** is a must-visit, celebrated by international guides as one of the world's most beautiful beaches. The sight from the golden cliffs is even more breathtaking in person, especially near the iconic double-arched rock that resembles a heart from above. This beach marks the beginning of the Algarve's best cliff-top walking trail, leading you past several other stunning beaches.

You can find comfortable accommodations at the Tivoli Carvoeiro in Lagoa.

- ***Praia do Camilo*** in Lagos is famed for its picture-perfect views from the wooden staircase that descends to the beach, enveloped by golden rock formations and featuring crystal-clear waters perfect for snorkeling. Despite its popularity and limited space, the beauty is undeniable. The beach is divided by a cliff with a connecting tunnel, revealing a larger area than initially apparent. Stay at the Cascade Wellness Resort for a luxurious experience.

- *Praia da Dona Ana,* overshadowed by the social media fame of Praia do Camilo, remains a sought-after spot in Lagos. Celebrated by international media as one of Portugal's best beaches, its cliffs, and rock formations provide shelter from the wind, with breathtaking views from the top. The Carvi Beach Hotel offers a nearby place to stay.

- *Prainha* is a romantic hideaway, featuring the quintessential Algarve landscape of coves and caves amidst towering rock formations. Often discovered by those wandering from the adjacent Três Irmãos beach, it's worth climbing the cliff for a panoramic view. The Prainha Clube is a great accommodation choice in Alvor.

- *Praia da Falésia,* likened to a "Grand Canyon by the sea," is one of the Algarve's longest beaches, backed by striking red and ochre cliffs. The view from the pine-clad cliffs is a must-see, and the proximity to excellent hotels like the Epic Sana Algarve in Albufeira makes it an ideal base for exploring the area.

- ***Ilha da Fuseta*** remains relatively unknown compared to Algarve's six sandy islands, primarily visited by locals. Accessible by boat from a quaint fishing village, it offers calm waters, especially towards the east, and miles of dunes. Consider staying at the Octant Vila Monte in Olhão.

- ***Praia de Cacela Velha,*** frequently featured in travel publications as one of the best in Europe and the world, retains a sense of undiscovered charm. This beach on one of the Ria Formosa Natural Park's islands are accessible from the picturesque village of Cacela Velha and are loved for its shallow waters and quiet, expansive stretches. It's a haven for families and naturists alike. The Robinson Club Quinta da Ria, located in Cacela Velha, provides nearby lodging.

- ***São Rafael Beach***
Ask around, and you'll hear some folks argue that São Rafael Beach, not Praia da Falésia, is Albufeira's

finest. It's a picture-perfect example of the Algarve, with its warm golden sands framed by striking ochre cliffs and formations. If you're up for adventure, you can explore the nearby grottoes and caves by kayak or paddleboard, or even on foot when the tide's right. Stick around for a breathtaking sunset from the cliff's edge. Plus, there are some top-notch hotels just a stone's throw away.

Location: Albufeira
Nearby Accommodations: São Rafael Atlântico

- *Arrifes Beach*
Catch Arrifes Beach at low tide and calm waters, and you're in for a treat—it's a gem of the Algarve. This cozy bay might fill up fast, but its stunning natural backdrop, with dramatic sea rocks and sheltering cliffs, is worth it. It's a hotspot for selfies, paddleboarding, and kayaking enthusiasts.
Location: Albufeira
Nearby Accommodations: São Rafael Suites

- *Benagil Beach*
Benagil Beach is famed for its spectacular sea cave, whichhas become a must-see in the Algarve, reachable only by boat. While it's not the place for solitude—thanks to its social media fame—you can still enjoy the clifftop walk will lead you to the stunning Praia da Marinha.
Location: Lagoa
Nearby Accommodations: Vale de Milho Village

- *Pinheiros Beach*

For those who love off-the-beaten-path spots, Pinheiros.

The beach is a hidden treasure at the base of a cliff. It's a bit of a hike down an unmarked trail, so it's mostly a younger, adventurous crowd that finds their way here. Its secluded nature has also made it a popular spot for nude sunbathing, with tranquil waters ideal for a swim.

Location: Lagos

Nearby Accommodations: Villas D. Dinis

- *Deserta Island*

Believe it or not, a desert island escape is just a hop away from the Algarve's largest city. Deserta Island is uninhabited, save for a solar-powered restaurant and a lighthouse. It's a pristine stretch of dunes and a 7km beach, often peaceful even during peak season. It's the go-to for undisturbed relaxation.

Location: Faro

Nearby Accommodations: Hotel Faro & Beach Club

- *Tavira Island*

Tavira Island, the most frequented of the Algarve's six islands, offers four distinct beaches. Arriving by ferry, you'll wander through pine forests to reach the sands, passing a campsite and eateries—the island's only structures. While it can get lively near these spots, a short walk reveals quieter, even secluded areas where nude sunbathing is common.

Location: Tavira

Nearby Accommodations: Vila Gale Albacora

- ***Carvalho Beach***
Straight out of a storybook, Carvalho Beach is accessed through a hidden tunnel and feels utterly enchanting. With its iconic sea rock
and cliffside "window," it's a secluded spot that's become popular for photos. For a tranquil visit, aim for late afternoon when the crowds thin
out.
Location: Lagoa

Nearby Accommodations: Pestana Palm Gardens

- ***Barril Beach***
Barril Beach is famed for its unique display of over 100 anchors in the dunes, remnants of a bygone fishing era. The old fishermen's cottages have been transformed into charming eateries. Reach this historical spot by walking over marshlands or taking a nostalgic train ride.
Location: Tavira
Nearby Accommodations: Pedras d'el Rei

- ***Armona Island***

Accessible by ferry year-round, Armona Island boasts a small fishing community. Stroll through the village street and over the dune boardwalk to find a beach with fine white sand that goes on for miles. The water is calm, clear, and shallow, and the further you walk, the more privacy you'll find. Keep an eye out for chameleons and birds among the dunes.

Location: Olhão
Nearby Accommodations: Real Marina Hotel

- ***João de Arens Beach***

João de Arens Beach was a well-kept secret until recently.
Tucked away at the bottom of a headland, it was a peaceful haven for the gay community. Now, it's beloved by all for its romantic setting and nude sunbathing. Before descending the trail, pause to take in the stunning cliffside view.

Location: Alvor
Nearby Accommodations: Villa Casa Da Guarda

- ***Barranco Beach***

A favorite among naturists and campers, Barranco Beach
remains a hidden gem to many. Its secluded location near Sagres, accessed via
an unpaved road, means fewer visitors and a preserved natural landscape of

green hills and cliffs. It's the perfect spot for a peaceful sunbathing away from
the surfer crowds.
Location: Sagres

Nearby Accommodations: Nature Beach Resort Quinta Al-Gharb

- ***Ninho de Andorinha Beach***
Tucked away among cliffs, this spot was once an accidental find during kayak excursions. But it's not just reachable by water – there's also a stairway carved into the cliffside. This charming nook is especially popular with lovebirds and the youth, who flock here to snap the ultimate shallow-water
selfies.
Location: Albufeira
Accommodations: Consider staying : Hotel Baia Grande.

- ***Odeceixe Beach***
Perched at the northern edge of the Algarve, this majestic beach boasts a picturesque locale where the Seixe River kisses the Atlantic.
Encased by the lush landscapes of the Sudoeste Alentejano e Costa Vicentina Natural Park, it's a haven for families on the gentler riverside and a hotspot for surfers braving the ocean's waves. Local surf schools are ready to gear you up and guide you. And if you're in search of a more secluded sunbathing session or prefer to sunbathe au naturel, sneak around to Praia das Adegas, the official

naturist cove, accessible at low tide or via a wooden stairway from the cliff.

Location: Costa Vicentina
Accommodations: Casas do Moinho is a cozy option.

SAILING FACTS ABOUT ALGARVE

Here, in the south of Portugal, is one of the best destinations in all of Europe for an unforgettable holiday. The Algarve has a proud reputation as a land of delicious cuisine, fascinating landscapes and villages, dreamy beaches, and year-round sunshine.

Every year thousands of holidaymakers travel to us, especially from Great Britain, because the journey time is only 2.5 hours. don't travel While everyone soon realizes what a great destination the Algarve is, not everyone is aware of its unique history.

six fascinating facts about the Algarve that even our neighbors in Portugal may not be aware of.

1. Algarve and #039; Michelin stars
The Algarve is known as a foodie's paradise. You'll find plenty of fresh seafood and produce, but some of Europe's most famous chefs have also set up their kitchens here.
There are currently 8 Michelin-starred restaurants in the Algarve. In 2022, A Ver Tavira and Al Sud were the last restaurants to receive a star at the Michelin Gala. Not only that, but restaurants Ocean and Vila Joya each received a second star this year.

2. Portugal's most famous cat
Although the head is unfortunately no longer with us because it disappeared years ago, Portugal's most famous cat once lived in the Algarve region. Mr. No Ears once amassed more than 20,000 followers on his social media profiles, who captured the one-eyed, speechless cat and his adventures on the streets of Albufeira.

Although Mr. No Ears has left planet Earth, his legacy lives on both at the cat shelter and in the book. Mr No Ears Cat Heaven was opened in his name by the non-profit association Associação Abrigo para Gatos Sr. With the support of Sem Orelhas, during Saudades Mr

No Ears's book reached hundreds of cat lovers all over Portugal.

3. Our history with Brazil. it is known that Portugal had a huge influence on Brazilian culture, and both countries share everything from language, food, and even architectural styles. But did you know that the Algarve was once part of the UK, along with Brazil and Portugal?

The United Kingdom of Portugal, Brazil, and the algarves was founded during the Napoleonic invasion of Portugal when the royal court was transferred to Brazil. When the State of Brazil was raised to the Kingdom of Brazil upon the arrival of the Portuguese court, a multicontinental monarchy
was established between the two countries in 1815.
It existed until 1822, when Brazil formally declared independence from Portugal, and finally dissolved. three years later, when the Kingdom of Brazil was recognized in 1925.

4. One of the most sparsely populated regions in Europe.
As popular as the Algarve is with vacationers who visit us every year, the region is surprisingly scarce when it comes to locals. of the population. The Algarve is one of the least populated regions in Europe, with around 76 inhabitants per

square kilometer. Compared to the UK, which has about 267 inhabitants per square kilometer, you can see why it is such a popular destination for British tourists!

5. Area of Natural Thermal Springs

Our area is known for its beautiful scenery, the cleanliness of our coast, and our rugged inland forests and natural parks. Less known to visitors is that the Algarve is an area with several natural thermal springs.

Fontes Naturais, as they are known locally, dot the Algarve and are a source of heated water known among locals for its healing powers. You will find several public swimming spots fed by springs from east to west of the area.

6. The region of Portugal with the most Blue Flag beaches

Finally, the Algarve may be famous for its sparkling beaches, but did you know that it is the region with the most Blue Flag beaches in all of Portugal? Over the years, the Algarve has maintained a consistently high reputation for the cleanliness, accessibility, safety, and environmental awareness of its beaches. In 2022, a total of 86 beaches and four marinas received the Blue Flag award.

CHAPTER FIVE

Shopping in the Algarve

 The best places to shop in the Algarve ranges from trendy malls with designer boutiques to traditional markets with local produce. No matter where you vacation in the area, you'll find a great spot for retail. InMaddition to Portuguese designer shops, you will also find international fashion brands and great places to buy handicrafts and fresh produce.

The Algarve's top shopping destinations feature unique architecture that blends local and cultural features with semi-open concepts. There are also wonderful places to have fun with an immersive film experience, children's workshops, outdoor concerts, and various events.

See our Algarve shopping picks below.

- **Mercado de LouléM Shopping** landmark in the hilltop town

Good for:
- Shopping
- Food
- Photo
- History
- Budget

Mercado   de Lolé in   the city   center.   It is the largest covered   market   in   southern Portugal. Founded in   1908,   the   market is one   of the number 39 attractions of the city, especially for its   architecture   that combines Moorish   and   Art Nouveau styles. Here you can expect various stalls selling a wide range of local products.

Here you can find gourmet and local products as well as fresh meat, seafood, and spices. Mercado de Loulé is also an excellent spot to sample traditional Portuguese   delicacies   and   beverages.   The handicrafts, textiles,   and ceramics on   display are enhanced   by the colorful landscapes. On Saturday, you can extend your visit to the shopping streets and cobblestone streets of the neighborhood with a farmer's market and a black market.

Location:
R. Al José Fernandes Guerreiro 34, 8100-535 Loulé, Portugal
Open: Monday to Saturday 7:00 a.m. to 10:30 p.m., Sundays 9:30 a.m. to 10:30 p.m.
Phone: +351 28 940 10280 8 4 44 40 Family-friendly shopping and leisure area

Suitable for:

• For shopping

• For families

• **MAR Shopping Algarve** is a large shopping and leisure center in Almancil. There are approximately 85 shops and eateries and 25 restaurants serving Algarve and international cuisine. There is also a laser cinema, an IKEA store, and Portugal's largest Primark.

If you have children with you, they can have hours of fun in the supervised indoor playground or the outdoor children's playground. The mall's outdoor area has water bodies and a miniature golf course. It also hosts regular events, including outdoor concerts. MAR Shopping Algarve is pet

friendly - you can leave your dog in Woof Land and enjoy shopping.
Location: Av. Algarve, 8135-182 Almancil, Portugal
Open: daily 9:00a/m-11:00p.m
Phone: +351 28 924 7842

* **Algarve Shopping**
Suitable for:

• For shopping

• For families
Algarve Shopping is a shopping center with more than 127 stores near Albufeira in Guia. Its most important brands are Zara, Fnac, Calzedonia, HandM, and Canda, as well as the large hypermarket Continente. Opened in 2011, the mall has a hint of Portuguese architecture thanks to its white, blue, and red facade. Other nearby shopping giants include Leroy Merlin, Nike Factory Store, and Casa Furniture Store.
Algarve Shopping is a cinema and dining area with 20 restaurants and cafes and highchairs are available for families with small children. Additional services and facilities include Wi-Fi, shoe repair, a dentist, a hairdresser, parking, and an adjacent car wash.

Location: Lanka Parque Comercial e Industrial do Algarve, Lote, R - Fração 3, 8201-878 Guia, Portugal

Open: Daily 8:00 AM - 11:00 PM

Phone: +351 28 910 5500

- ***Aqua Portimão Shopping Center***

Wide range of modern shopping centers
Suitable for:

• Shopping

• Food

• Families

Aqua Portimão Shopping Center is one of the most modern shopping centers in Portimão. It opened over a decade ago and has been steadily attracting locals and tourists ever since. There are two floors of shops and a charming dining area on the top floor. Large semi-open spaces with lots of greenery create a pleasant shopping experience.

Aqua Portimao shopping center has approximately 120 stores with well known brands such Desigual, Decathlon, Mango, Pull and Bear and Foot Locker.

The shopping center regularly organizes events and activities, such as workshops for children on weekends.
Location: R. de São Pedro 72, 8500-448 Portimão, Portugal
Open: Saturday 10:00a.m-12:30p.m, Sunday-Friday 10:00a.m-11:00p.m
Algarve: +351 28 241 444 444

• **Large shopping center near Faro Airport**
Goods:
• Shoppers
• Food
• Families
Forum Algarve is a large shopping center located on the main road near Faro Airport. The 45,000 square meter complex and architectural style includes elements specific to the area and a multitude of open spaces. Here you will find stores of several important brands such as Guess, Mango, Cortefiel, Nespresso, and Apple.

For entertainment, Forum Algarve has a cinema with 5 screens. When it comes to dining, you can choose from more than 20 restaurants and cafes serving traditional Portuguese and international cuisine. There is also a shuttle service from Faro Airport to the luggage storage, allowing you to shop before your flight.

Location:
8005-445 Faro, Portugal
Open: Daily 10am-11pm
Phone: +351 28 988 9300

- *Mercados de Olhão*

Excellent source of fresh Algarve produce:
• Budget

Mercados de Olhão is a municipal market that has existed since 1915. The market is easily recognizable by its red brick walls and towers and consists of two buildings. One includes a wide variety of seafood. The vendors are friendly, so don't be afraid to ask the locals for cooking tips.
The second building has stalls selling seasonal fruit and vegetables selected from the Algarve region. If you come on a Saturday, you'll find cheeses, olives, dried fruits, and nuts from local producers near this indoor market.

Location: Mercados Municipais, Av. 5 de Outubro, 8700-412 Olhão, Portugal
Open: Monday to Friday 7:00 a.m. to 2:00 p.m., Saturdays 7:00 a.m. to
1:00 p.m. (closed on Sundays)

Phone: +351 28 024 41 94

- **Stylish shopping destination**

Suitable for:
- Shopping

• Budget

Designer Outlet Algarve is an outdoor outlet in Almancil, about 20 20-minute drive from Faro. Established in 2017, a typical local village with more than 60 shops now. You can expect discounts of 30-70% on the biggest international and Portuguese brands. The most prominent brands of Designer Outlet Algarves are Adidas, Timberland, Guess, Levi's, Hugo Boss, Calvin Klein and Bimba y Lola. It's a great place to window shop and find great deals on fashion, children's clothing, accessories, outdoor clothing, shoes, and homewares.
Location: Av. Algarve, 8135-182 Almancil, Portugal
Open: Daily 10am - 1pm
PHONE: +351 28 924 6000

• MERCODO da Fonte Santa, Quarteira
and Gipsy Market da Fonte Santa, also known as Quarteira Gypsy Market, is located in Quarteira in the suburbs. This Wednesday flea market is a great place to find good finds. You will find a selection of typical flea market products such as clothing, bedding, handbags, and cork products.

Visit when the weather is nice to browse more vendors and trinkets. Mercado da Fonte Santa has a

convenient parking lot. Alternatively, you can get there by taking the green
route bus from Vilamoura.

Location: EM527-2 621A, 8125-020 Quarteira, Portugal

Open: Wednesday 8:00 AM - 2:00 PM (Closed Thursday -Tuesday)

- **Faro Municipal Market**

Shoppers

• Food

• Budget

Faro City Market is an indoor market popular with locals and visitors for its wide range of fresh produce. This market is located in the center of Faro in a white building with a tower in the middle. Come here to fill your basket to prepare for a picnic or a great dinner. markets are full of colorful vegetables, delicious fruits, high-quality meat, and various seafood. You can also find home-baked breads and pastries. If you're feeling peckish, just go for lunch at one of the surrounding restaurants or enjoy a delicious local beer at a local cafe.

Location: Largo Dr. Francisco Sa Carneiro, 8000-151 Faro, Portugal
Open: daily 7:00 a.m. - midnight

Phone: +351 28 989 7250

- **Albufeira Shopping**

Compact and convenient shopping in a coastal town
Good for:

• Shopping

• Food

Albufeira Shopping is a fairly compact shopping center with a supermarket and about 40 shops selling products at reasonable prices. Like any mall, you can find almost everything from clothing and sportswear to home decor and electronics.
The mall has temporary pop-up shops from local producers. There is also a food court where you can enjoy pizza and Asian delicacies, as well as several cafes and bakeries. Shopping at Albufeira is a convenient place to buy essentials if you want to

cook for yourself or find goods and souvenirs to bring home.

Location: Lote, R. do Município 32, 8200-161 Albufeira, Portugal
Open: daily 8:00 - 22:00
Phone: +351 28 959 8430

DELICIOUS DISHES TO ENJOY IN PORTUGAL

Algarve beaches, hidden coves, and postcard-style villages bleached where traditional taverns prepare delicious delicacies from simple grilled sardines drizzled with olive oil and lemon juice. Don't miss these dishes, from delicious fish and shellfish to sun-baked vegetables and flame-grilled meats...

1. Couvert
Although not a dish in itself, many meals in Portugal begins with a couvert or appetizer. It can be as simple as a bowl of olives, bread, or a selection of cheeses, although pickled carrots are also popular. Try making your own by lightly boiling

sliced carrots for up   to 10   minutes before tossing with olive oil, white wine, and garlic and chilling in the fridge. Add parsley to serve.

2. Conquilhas à Algarvia
Succulent mussels fresh from the sea take center stage in this signature Algarve dish. You can recreate it by pan-frying onions, garlic, and sliced Portuguese sausage before adding clams and garnishing with parsley or coriander. Remember to wash the clams thoroughly in cold water to remove the grit, and never eat them unopened. Enjoy traditional marisco (shellfish) dishes or small plates of queijo and cod ceviche against the blue-and-white tiles of Lagos' simple Tasca Jota. Cataplana de marisco

If you just can't get enough seafood, be sure to seek out the cataplana de marisco, a daily feast of lobster, clams, squid, and everything in between. All lightly fried with herbs, white wine, and tomatoes and served with the resulting heavenly liqueur. The rustic Restaurant a Barrigada offers plenty of seafood, with a prix fixe buffet of premium grilled sardines, octopus, and prawns served with a simple salad and garlic fries. Just 100 meters from Lagos Beach, the hotel is also the perfect place to watch the boats in the marina.

3. Petiscos de Taberna

Be sure to stop at Petiscos de Taberna while wandering the winding streets of Lagos. Similar to Spanish tapas, these snacks are best enjoyed with a chilled glass of locally made cervejo. Expect small meat sandwiches, usually slices of pork or beef, seafood, and chouriço. Sausage is king in Portugal and there are many festivals dedicated to it. Don't miss the Feira dos Enchidos Tradicionais in nearby Monchique. At the beginning of March, an endless selection of sausages and a meeting of artisan producers are organized.

4. Feijoada

You could be forgiven for thinking Algarve food consists of fish, but you can also find feijoada, This hearty bean stew typically combines pork, beans, cured meat, veggies, and seasonings. Offals such as ears and trotters can also be used, but you can be sure they will be tasty. Try it in the sheltered garden of No Patio, a popular Brazilian/European restaurant in Lagos.

5. Dom Rodrigos
Cakes and pastries are very popular all over Portugal, but Dom Rodrigos is a specialty of the Algarve. These beautiful nests are usually made of colorful leaf wrappers made from egg yolks (egg yolks finished with syrup or "angel hair"), egg yolk, cinnamon, and almonds.

6. Leitão
Few things are more satisfying than finding a restaurant that serves leitão, a pig smothered in herbs and roasted on its lap for up to 24 hours. The suckling pigs are only a few weeks old and after slow cooking, the meat is tender and the skin is crispy.

7. Caldo Verde

This frugal but satisfying soup originated in northern Portugal, but is less indulgent than suckling pig, but is now a national dish. The main ingredients are potatoes and kale, but bacon and sausage can be added for extra flavor. The beauty of this caldo verde is that it can easily be recreated at home.

8. Queijo
Portugal produces fine cheeses rarely seen in Britain. The desert landscape makes it

ideal for raising sheep and goats, and their milk is used to
make a variety of hard and soft cheeses. Enjoy them on their own, with chewy pão de queijo (cheese bread) or bread and sweet, locally produced pumpkin jam. For fine dining, try the marmelada de abóbora e Salada de espinafres (pumpkin jam and spinach salad) with goat cheese, a local specialty served
at the Artistas restaurant in Lagos' old town.

9. Wine

The four regions of the Algarve - Lagos, Portimão, Lagoa, and Tavira - have their distinct wine varieties, all guaranteed Denominação de Origem Controlada status. Bathed in sunshine for most of the year, the region produces everything from light, refreshing whites to fish and full-bodied reds, perfect for stews and cured meats. If you need a fire, explore the back streets of Lagos past the marina, where locals linger over glasses of Aguardente de Medronho, a strong brandy made from the fruit of the Arbutus tree.

CHAPTER SIX

Is the Algarve safe? Top safety tips for the Algarve

Is the Algarve safe?
What are the biggest risks that tourists should be aware of in the Algarve?

Portugal is regarded as one of the world's safest countries, with low crime rates and pleasant residents. However, it's always important to be careful when I have provided a full overview of crime rates and included some tips to keep you safe while visiting the Algarve. After reading, you will feel much more confident about visiting one of Portugal's most popular tourist destinations!

Is the Algarve safe?

The Algarve is generally considered very safe, especially compared to other tourist destinations around the world.

As with any travel destination, common sense is your friend. Pickpocketing can happen in crowded tourist areas, so keep your belongings safe and aware of your surroundings. In terms of personal safety, violent crimes are extremely rare, especially against tourists in the Algarve.

The most common problem encountered by visitors to the Algarve is petty theft, mainly from unattended cars and hotel rooms. To protect it, do not leave valuables in the car, and keep valuables well hidden if you do not intend to take them with you.

In short, although the Algarve is safe, it is always best to be vigilant and follow the usual travel safety precautions.

Where is Algarve Portugal on the map?

The Algarve is located in the southernmost region of Portugal, bordering the Atlantic Ocean to the south and west. If you imagine Portugal on a map, it is the bottom piece that covers the entire width of the country.

This is a popular area known for its stunning coastline, picturesque fishing towns, and world-class golf courses. The Algarve is also home to Faro, the capital of the region and gateway to many tourists thanks to its international airport, and the ever-popular Lagos, iconic for its sea caves! The area is easy to travel by car, and all major towns and attractions are connected by a well-maintained road network. Whether you want to relax on the beach, explore the culture, or enjoy the local cuisine, the Algarve is a great destination.

Safety tips for visitors to the Algarve

These tips are intended to make you aware of potential safety issues and should cause you any anxiety before your visit. As I mentioned, the Algarve region of Portugal is very safe, but every tourist destination has its share of things to be aware of.

1. Be alert in crowded places: Keep a close eye on your belongings in crowded places because theft can happen. This is especially important in tourist areas or public transport.

2. Protect valuables: Keep valuables well-hidden when you are not carrying them with you. Use a safe in your hotel room if you have one (if it's bolted down) or keep everything well-hidden if you don't (NOT under the mattress!)

3. Avoid showing off wealth: It's wise to avoid expensive jewelry, cameras, or other valuables showing off, which can make you a target for

thieves. If you're walking around with an expensive camera, always travel with a guy who's focused on you, or stay away from crowded places. The Algarve is more expensive than other popular destinations, but it's still not a good idea to spread the word.

4. Travel with certified tour operators. Make sure you always use licensed and trusted tour operators for activities such as boat
trips or guided tours.

5. Road safety: When driving, remember that the Portuguese drive on the right side of the road. Always obey the speed limit and never drive drunk.

6. Beach safety: Pay attention to flag warnings on the beach. A red flag means that swimming is not safe due to strong currents or rough seas.

7. Moisturize and wear sunscreen: The Algarve can get very hot, especially in summer. Stay hydrated and apply sunscreen regularly, even if the weather is cloudy.

8. Learn basic Portuguese phrases: Although most locals speak English, knowing a few basic Portuguese phrases can be useful and appreciated, especially in an emergency.

9. Respect local customs: Portuguese people tend to be conservative. Dress

modestly, especially when visiting religious sites, and respect local customs.

10. Emergency contact information: Keep a list of emergency numbers. The general emergency number in Portugal is 112.
In this section, we'll address some frequently asked questions regarding the safety of the Algarve region in Portugal, and I'll provide plenty of helpful insights on how to keep safe while enjoying your stay!

Is it safe for Americans to visit the Algarve?

Absolutely! The Algarve welcomes visitors from across the globe, including Americans. Though the local culture may differ from what you're accustomed to back home, the area is renowned for its friendly residents With good tourism facilities. English is widely spoken, especially in areas frequented by tourists, and the infrastructure is modern and well-kept.
Just be sure to respect local traditions, stay alert, and secure your items.

Can I feel secure in the Algarve during the night?

Yes, the Algarve is generally secure after dark. You'll find a vibrant nightlife scene in hotspots like Albufeira, Vilamoura, and Lagos, brimming with a variety of bars, clubs, and eateries. Still, it's smart to take basic safety measures: stay in illuminated areas, avoid solitary walks in isolated spots, and watch your beverages. It's also smart to arrange your ride back to where you're staying in advance. And a word to the wise: always keep a close eye on your drink, as unfortunately, date rape drugs are a concern across Europe.

Does the Algarve have a high rate of violent crime?

Portugal is often listed among the world's safest countries,
and the Algarve reflects this with a low rate of violent crime. Most incidents
involve minor theft rather than anything more serious.

Is Portugal safe for U.S. citizens?

Yes, Portugal is generally a safe destination for the U.S. citizens, with a modern infrastructure and a high-quality healthcare system.
English is widely spoken, particularly in tourist regions. Just like any international travel, stay vigilant in crowded places and keep your belongings close. But overall, the risk for American tourists in Portugal is minimal.

Is the Algarve a safe place to live?

Indeed, the Algarve is considered a safe place to reside,
with a friendly local community and a low incidence of violent crime. The
standard of living is high, with modern amenities and a solid healthcare

system. There's also a sizeable expat community for support. Just remember to
explore different neighborhoods to find the right fit for you and consider
learning some Portuguese to enhance your experience.

Is it safe to travel around the Algarve?

Yes, traveling around the Algarve is safe, whether by rental car, public transit, or flight. The roads are well-maintained, Public transportation is effective as well as trustworthy. If you're driving, remember to keep your valuables out of sight and doors locked. Faro Airport is the main hub for the region, offering a modern and secure gateway to this tourist favorite.

How safe is public transportation in the Algarve?

Public transportation in the Algarve is safe and a great way to see the area. However, remain vigilant against pickpockets, particularly on buses and trains, and be cautious at bus stops and stations at night. Despite these concerns, public transit remains a fantastic way to immerse yourself in
the local culture.

Should I consider visiting the Algarve?

Definitely! The Algarve is a safe destination with a focus
on tourist safety. With clear procedures to handle safety concerns, you can
relax and enjoy what this beautiful region has to offer.

The folks in the Algarve are a friendly bunch, and most who
come to visit have a smooth and enjoyable time. Ensure to constantly maintain an eye on your stuff and stay safe, as you would anywhere else. But don't worry, the
The Algarve is an awesome place for a vacation.

Wondering about Albufeira? It's a safe bet for travelers.
Known for its lively nightlife, stunning beaches, and quaint old town, Albufeira is a hit with tourists and keeps things secure with diligent local authorities. Just use your noggin and watch out for your belongings, especially when the sun sets or in bustling spots. But fear not, nearly everyone who heads to Albufeira has a blast without any hitches.

How about Faro?

Yep, Faro's safe too. Sure, being the Algarve's capital might see a bit more crime than quieter spots, but it's mostly just small-time stuff like pickpocketing. Stay sharp and you'll have a fab time exploring Faro's history, charming streets, and nearby beaches. Plus, the police there have got your back.

And the Algarve beaches?

They're safe as houses but do keep an eye on your beach bag and the waves. These beaches are clean and family-friendly, and come summer, there's usually a lifeguard keeping watch.

Remember to follow the flag warnings for swimming conditions, watch out for strong currents if you've got little ones, and slap on that sunscreen.

Thinking about natural disasters? The Algarve's pretty chill in that department. Portugal does have some fault lines, but earthquakes are rare. You might see some flooding if the heavens open up in winter, and forest fires can happen up north in the summer, but overall, the Algarve's not a hotspot for major natural disasters.

Do folks speak English?

Absolutely. With tourists from all corners of the globe, you'll find plenty of English speakers, especially in the service industry. But hey, learning a few Portuguese phrases can make your trip even cooler. I'm all about Duolingo for learning on the fly.

Now, what should tourists watch out for? Keep your wits about you for small-time crimes like theft, especially where it's crowded or on public transport. If you're driving, get to know the local road rules and make sure your rental's in good nick. Don't forget, the sun's no joke – protect your skin, stay hydrated, and go easy on the booze. And at the beach, always swim safe – heed the flags and be mindful of the ocean's mood.

Stick to these tips, and you're all set for a fabulous time in the Algarve.

The Algarve, nestled in the sun-kissed southern tip of Portugal is famous not just for its gorgeous beaches and dramatic scenery, but also for its vibrant and colorful festivities that bring out the area's rich heritage and culinary delights. If you find yourself around Figs on the Funcho, you're in for a treat, as you'll be right in the heart of these exuberant celebrations.

Come February, the Carnival Parade is the talk of the town, with the grandest spectacle in Loule. Yet, Carvoerio and Alte also throw their lively parades, so there's plenty of merriment to go around. Just remember, Loulé's carnival is ticketed, so plan to get there early and maybe catch a bite before the show kicks off.

When Easter rolls around, Loule becomes a hub of spiritual celebration with the Festival of the Sovereign Mother. Spanning two weeks, it starts with the Festa Pequena, where the revered image of the Sovereign Mother is paraded to São Francisco Church to stay for the festival. The festivities culminate two weeks later with the grand Festa Grande.

Beer aficionados, mark your calendars for July's Beer Festival in Silves. This multi-day bash serves up a plethora of brews, both boozy and non-alcoholic, complemented by an array of delicious eats from various stalls. To top it off, live bands and singers set the mood with their performances.

Fast forward to August, and you're transported back in time at the Silves Medieval Festival. Wander the streets to the castle and you'll find yourself amidst BBQs, spit roasts, and entertainers. The market stalls are treasure troves of Moroccan wares, handmade arts, and sparkling jewelry.

The sizzle of July and August brings the much-anticipated Annual Sardine Festival. On the beach promenade of Olhos d'Agua, you can indulge in sizzling, freshly grilled sardines. This event is popular with both locals and visitors.

And as the year wraps up, Albufeira's New Year's Party on Fishermen's Beach is legendary for its summery beach bashes and concerts. With international artists and bands joining the lineup, it's an unforgettable way to ring in the new year.

In essence, the Algarve's lineup of festivals is a smorgasbord of the religious, the cultural, and the epicurean, offering a little something for everyone's tastes.

MAP

Printed in Great Britain
by Amazon

43794495R00066